D1336892

3 8014 07042 0812

David
Bowie

David Bowie

Jeff Hudson

endeavour

David Bowie is part of the series of books on Hollywood and Rock Icons.
The design was initiated by Paul Welti, but created by Ros Holder.
Author Jeff Hudson worked closely with picture researcher Jennifer Jeffrey.
The book was edited by Mark Fletcher. Mary Osborne led the production.

Endeavour London Ltd
21-31 Woodfield Road
London W9 2BA

ISBN 978-1-873913-33-8

Printed and bound in Singapore
1 3 5 7 9 10 8 6 4 2

Frontispiece: David Bowie
in the spotlight on his Reality
tour, September 24, 2002, at Le
Zenith in Paris, France.
Title Page: Ziggy Stardust in
his Kansai Yamamoto robe,
Earls Court, London, May 12,
1973. The Chinese script spells
out "David Bowie" and not, as
Bowie said in 1999, "Get your
potatoes here"!

Above: Bowie performing to fan
club members in his "Angel of Death"
costume at London's Marquee Club,
recorded for the TV show *Midnight
Special*, October 21, 1973.

Contents

Chapter 1

The Rise and Fall of David Jones

"I left Brixton when I was still quite young, but that was enough to be very affected by it. It left strong images in my mind."

Future Legend

David Bowie wasn't born. He was *created*. The story begins in Brixton, south-east London, where David Robert Jones arrived on January 8, 1947, to Haywood "John" Jones and Peggy Burns (they married later that year). Everyone is a product of their background, but young David seemed to devour influences like other children hunted sweets. From Peggy he took a sense of the theatrical and, she claims, the Burns family's gift for singing. From his father David saw how non-confrontation often won the day, later surrounding himself with others to do his bidding. Even the family's new home in Bromley, Kent, where he lived from six years old, saw a fascination with suburbia flourish alongside David's resentful distaste for being so distant from London. In truth, the capital was only a short train ride away, and David and elder step-brother Terry were regular visitors. But he took from Bromley a sense of being on the outside—a location he seems to have inhabited mentally ever since.

Young David was not a great student (he would leave Bromley Technical High School with one O level qualification—in art) but his musical education was second to none. Terry's love of Charles Mingus and John Coltrane became David's love as well, all reproduced on his first plastic saxophone. Peggy's music-hall favorites and TV stars like Anthony Newley and Danny Kaye were soaked up with the same enthusiasm. But it was when Haywood Jones brought home a collection of American rock 'n' roll 45s that David found what he'd been searching for. "I had heard God," he recalls. And his name was Little Richard.

It was a natural step to join a band, although The Konrads, and later, The King Bees and The Manish Boys, showed nothing of the eclecticism—or talent—for which he would become known. In fact, an incident at school did more to shape his future fame than any musical achievement. A punch in the face (in an argument over a girl) by his ring-wearing friend, George Underwood, left Jones' left eye with a permanently dilated pupil. To the casual observer he appeared to have different colored eyes.

The first part of the Bowie legend was in place.

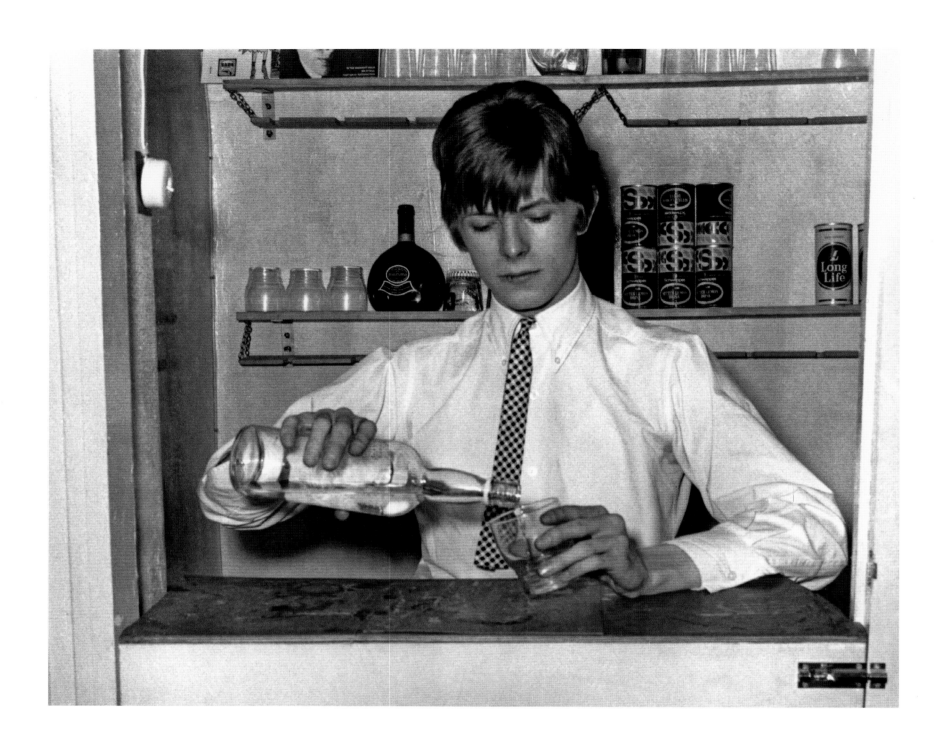

Opposite: The perfect cocktail in the making. His early bands were fairly pedestrian rock 'n' roll, but in his head Jones was equal measures Danny Kaye, Anthony Newley, and Little Richard.

Left: Whether it was playing modern jazz or music hall on his first plastic saxophone or working out the latest rock 'n' roll riffs on this Framus twelve-string guitar, the young David Jones just wanted to play.

Fame

If *American Idol* had been around in the 1960s, David Jones would have been one of the thousands lining up to audition. This was a boy with a thirst for fame and an energy to make it happen. And he didn't mind how.

A cheeky letter to entrepreneur John Bloom, inviting investment, found its way to Doris Day's publisher, Leslie Conn. In June 1964, with Conn as manager, Davie Jones & The King Bees released their first single, "Liza Jane"—to total public apathy. Undaunted, Jones' next major appearance combined his joint loves of fashion—and being noticed. The BBC's *Tonight* show was a respectable news program, but somehow presenter Cliff Michelmore found himself interviewing David Jones in his capacity as President of The Society For The Prevention Of Cruelty To Long-Haired Men. Jones had never been happier.

Left: What's in a name? Everything. Could David Bowie have fronted The Konrads, Davie Jones have written "Life On Mars?" or Dave Jay have invented The Thin White Duke? Only David Jones knows the answer.

Right: Although teacher and occasional lover Lindsay Kemp (*inset*) says, "I didn't really teach him to be a mime artiste but to be more of himself on the outside", the effects of those lessons are visible every time Bowie steps on stage.

Dancing with the Big Boys

After The King Bees came The Lower Third and a new manager, Ken Pitt. Pitt's background was more variety than rock 'n' roll—which suited Jones' desire to be an all-round entertainer like his hero, Danny Kaye. A typical Lower Third gig, after all, featured songs from Holst, Rodgers & Hammerstein, and *Mary Poppins*.

Jones didn't want just to sing. He wanted to *perform*. Impressing in Soho dance classes run by mime artiste Lindsay Kemp led to a part in Kemp's touring show, *Pierrot In Turquoise*, during which he danced and performed his own songs. He would later reprise this act, supporting his friend Marc Bolan.

But he wouldn't do it as himself. Future Monkee Davy Jones was already a famous actor, Pitt said. A new name was needed.

And David Bowie was born.

"There's no point in being in this business if nobody knows you."

Watch That Man

If David Jones had seemed hell-bent on fame then there was absolutely nothing that his alter ego Bowie would not do. New bands The Buzz and Riot Squad came and went, a rock opera, *Ernie Johnson*, was composed (unrecorded), he wrote a play for the BBC (*The Champion Flower Grower*—rejected), and failed auditions for various films, including *Virgin Soldiers* (although he won work as an extra). But he did appear in a TV commercial for Lyons Maid ice cream. He was selected by Lindsay Kemp to dance in a BBC play (alongside future girlfriend Hermione Farthingale). And he did release his first solo album.

Called *David Bowie* and released on the same day as *Sgt. Pepper...*, the album surprised everyone who heard it. Certainly fans of The Lower Third or any of his other R&B incarnations would not have recognized the fourteen quirky music hall tunes sung in an odd "cockney" accent. There was macabre theater in "Please Mr. Gravedigger", a hint at cross-dressing in "She's Got Medals", and actual waltzes in "Maid Of Bond Street". Arguably it is a single not included on the album which best sums up Bowie's thinking at the time. "The Laughing Gnome", featuring bad puns and sped-up dialogue from Bowie and engineer Gus Dudgeon, would later be disowned by the singer—despite reaching Number 3 in the UK in 1973.

However, it was another collaboration with Dudgeon, this time with him as producer, which gave Bowie his first hit. It was 1969, Neil Armstrong was about to set foot on the Moon, and David Bowie released "Space Oddity". The countdown to fame had begun.

Left and above: Bowie channeled everything into his music, forming a group called Feathers just to be able to play alongside girlfriend Hermione, and gigging wherever he could (he popped up as a backup singer for The Strawbs on a BBC2 TV show). He even won two contests in Malta, where he was holidaying with manager and rumored lover Pitt, with his performances of "When I Live My Dream".

Opposite: With his promoter hat firmly on, Bowie transformed Beckenham's weekly folk club meetings into The Arts Lab—an experimental gathering of the latest talents. The Lab's greatest success was captured on "Memory Of A Free Festival", the closing track on his second album.
Left: At the *Disc* and *Music Echo* Valentine Awards ceremony at the Café Royal in London, February 1970.

P9762

P9763

Opposite: With fellow MainMan-produced singer, the former British water-skiing champion, Dana Gillespie, May 17, 1971.
Left: The sound of 1970's *The Man Who Sold The World* was early heavy metal—but Bowie's image at the time was anything but, as this Los Angeles gathering discovered.

I Know It's Gonna Happen Someday

If Bowie's first album had been a quirky take on music hall, the second, called *David Bowie* in the UK but *Man Of Words, Man Of Music* in the US (1969), was little more than melodic folk. Songs like "Wild Eyed Boy From Free Cloud" and "Memory Of A Free Festival" hint at a nascent skill for writing powerful hooks but the vocals are unrecognizable from those of the superstar-to-be. Yet, in "Janine", with its references to the singer hiding his true identity behind another character, we get a glimpse of things to come. And, of course, through the emergence of "Major Tom", he gave us the first fully-fledged Bowie alter ego.

However, despite the success of "Space Oddity", and Bowie's first appearance—with his Stylophone—on the UK's *Top Of The Pops* program, the LP and further singles failed to attract attention. He had tried music hall and folk. What was left?

"I don't wear dresses all the time. I change every day. I'm not outrageous. I'm David Bowie."

Be My Wife

Bowie would later cite his confession of bisexuality as "the biggest mistake I ever made"—for the simple reason that it alienated a lot of potential markets, in particular the all-important American media. But there was no denying he made the most of his appeal to both sexes. His relationship with Lindsay Kemp had foundered when the choreographer discovered Bowie was also seeing costume designer Natasha Korniloff. Ken Pitt, another of Bowie's rumored partners, was forced to share his lover with a succession of girls. After Hermione came journalist Mary Finnigan, co-founder of The Arts Lab, but

it was another Mary who made the greatest impression.

Mary Angela Barnett, or "Angie" as she was known, was an explosion of energy and attitude. Typically colorful, she recalls meeting David when "we were both fucking the same bloke." But something clicked between them. Angie wanted fame as much for him as she did for herself, and her own bisexuality, fashion instincts, and liberal morals were just what Bowie needed. They married on March 19, 1970, when Angie permanently took Bowie as her last name (although legally the singer is still called "Jones"). A year later she would

bear David their first child, Zowie.

But as Bowie found one soulmate he was about to lose another. The Jones family had never been openly tactile, but David's love for his father was immense. Their shared characteristics were numerous and the father/son bond, forged over their love of US music, had always given him strength. So when Bowie returned from a trip to Malta with Ken Pitt to discover John Jones at death's door with lobal pneumonia, he was devastated.

Jones Snr. died on August 5, 1969, just weeks before "Space Oddity" would set his son on course to become a star.

Left: The boy from suburbia. The glam rocker at his rented home, Haddon Hall, in 1972. It was paid for by the royalties from "Space Oddity".

You Belong in Rock 'n' Roll

From the outside, David Bowie seems to have encouraged confrontation. His long-hair campaign is a case in point. But even for a performer with such thick skin, the sound of a thousand northern kids booing his hippy folk act in 1969 proved hard to take. If there is a definite point when he decided to "hide" from his audience, then that night on October 24, supporting Humble Pie at the Sunderland Empire, is probably it.

He was not going to give up performing, but he needed to find a way to protect himself. He found the answer with his next project: The Hype.

The Hype looked like an early version of glam rock but the band actually served a different purpose: it gave Bowie a part to play and a role to hide behind. If people heckled now, it wasn't at him, it

was at his character "Rainbowman". Tony Visconti was Hypeman, drummer John Cambridge was Cowboyman and, arriving at the last minute, was Cambridge's old Hull friend on guitar, Gangsterman—otherwise known as Mick Ronson. The band recorded a BBC session for John Peel on February 5, 1970, then played their first gig a fortnight later in full superhero garb.

Egged on by Angie and his growing confidence, Bowie made other changes. Manager Ken Pitt was replaced by Tony Defries's MainMan company, while home became a rambling Victorian building in Bromley, its rent paid for entirely by the royalties from "Space Oddity". From here, surrounded by the imposing influences of Angie, and dozens of passing friends, Bowie would plot his

world domination. And the first stage was *The Man Who Sold The World*.

Any of the half-dozen people who had bought the previous albums would have been shocked by this one. Despite the cover featuring Bowie reclining on a chaise longue in a dress, the lank-haired hippy from the 1960s was replaced by an angry heavy metaller, years ahead of his time. Aided by Ronson's arrangements and Visconti's production, Bowie raged through brother Terry's mental illness in "All The Madmen" and Vietnam War atrocities in "Running Gun Blues" and Nietzschean imperatives in "The Supermen". Even the title track, emotively covered by Nirvana later, features Bowie in anguished, impenetrable conversation with himself.

What was he going to do next?

Shapes of Things

The Man Who Sold The World sold reasonably in the US but hardly at all in Bowie's home country. As a result, Bowie's deal with Mercury Records was allowed to lapse. Undaunted and inspired, he embarked on a marathon songwriting and recording period which would produce enough material for two albums—if he could find someone to release them.

On September 9, 1971, Bowie flew to New York to sign a three-album deal with the American giant RCA—home among others to Elvis, with whom Bowie shares a birthday—worth $37,500. The company had been impressed by some of the new sounds coming from Trident Studios. They were not the only ones.

Released in December 1971, *Hunky Dory* took many of Bowie's cultural obsessions and dressed them up in the perfect pop arrangements. From the opening song, "Changes", with its catchy faux stutter masking a dismissal of rock stardom to a return to Nietzschean thinking in "Oh! You Pretty Things", via the bleak landscape of "Life On Mars?", each track reveals a thoughtful gem of a lyric wrapped in eminently palatable melodies. While "Queen Bitch", "Andy Warhol", and "Song For Dylan" were paeans to Bowie's heroes (Lou Reed being the "Bitch"), and "The Bewley Brothers" coming close to autobiography, it was "Kooks" which really connected. "I was in the studio listening to Neil Young when I got the call that my son had been born," Bowie recalls. "So I wrote 'Kooks' for him."

Apart from Yes keyboard player Rick Wakeman, the album's musicians were Trevor Bolder on bass, drummer Mick "Woody" Woodmansey, and Ronson. Nobody knew at the time but The Spiders from Mars had arrived.

Left: Mick Ronson had all but given up on music, especially any hope of breaking into the London scene, when friend John Cambridge called him back from Hull to join Bowie's new band, The Hype. He played on a reworking of "Memory Of A Free Festival", but it was his blistering guitar work on *The Man Who Sold The World* that caught the ear.

Above: February 24, 1972, Wallington Public Hall, Surrey. With Bowie's imagination and Ronson's technique, people said they could conquer the world. And with The Spiders from Mars they did.

Chapter 2

Golden Years

Above: "I'm not bloody wearing that!" were drummer Woodmansey's words when The Spiders' costumes arrived. But it was a different story, Bowie recalls, "when they realized the girls were going crazy for them because they looked like no one else."

Left: The age of the androgynous glam rocker had arrived.

Previous page: The longer the Ziggy Stardust/Aladdin Sane tour went on, the harder it became for Bowie to shake off his character each night.

Opposite: Crystal Japan—swaddled in sumo garb for Ziggy's first visit to Japan, April 1973.
Left: June 1, 1973, at St. George's Hall, Bradford.

Changes

It began with a haircut.

In early January 1972 David Bowie walked into the Evelyn Page salon in Beckenham and showed a photograph to young stylist Suzy Fussey. "That's how I want to look." It didn't matter to him, or her, that the picture in question was of a female catwalk model wearing the latest Kansai Yamamoto design. Two weeks later, as increased media coverage of Yamamoto's first London show gave him fresh ideas, Bowie returned to Suzy with new instructions. "I had her cut my hair in early January 1972," Bowie recalls. "No dye. Laid flattish. I believe my hair went red and stood up between the twentieth and twenty-fifth of January 1972."

Ziggy's look was born. Now he needed the sound to match.

Who Can I Be Now

Everything fell into place with the release of *The Rise And Fall Of Ziggy Stardust And The Spiders From Mars* in June 1972. The band that had been touring and recording together for months—Ronson, Woodmansey, and Bolder—took a name: The Spiders. And Bowie, after experimenting lyrically with a variety of viewpoints and characters, finally discovered a mask that fitted perfectly.

He *was* Ziggy Stardust.

But the album could have been so different had Mott The Hoople recorded the first song Bowie offered them in 1972 instead of "All The Young Dudes"—a number called "Suffragette City"—and if the single he'd released the previous year under the name Arnold Corns—"Moonage Daydream"/"Hang Onto Yourself"—had become even a minor hit.

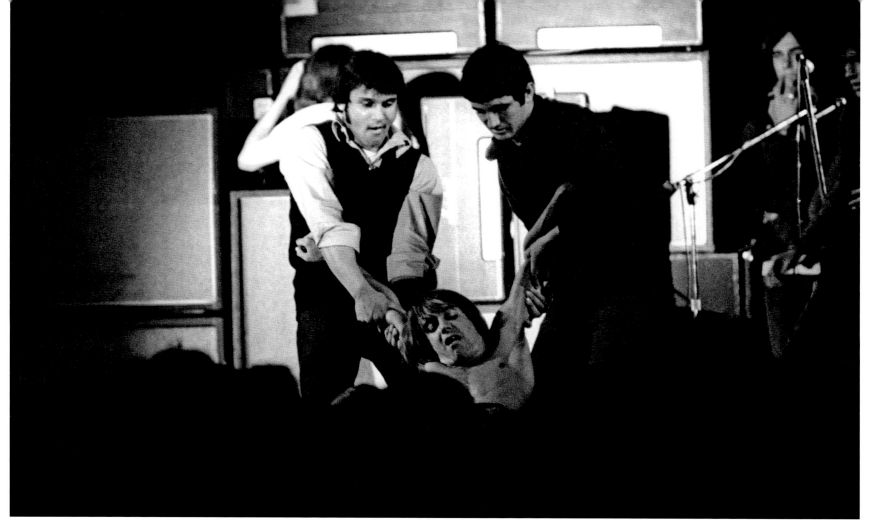

Left: Entrancing the north of England on January 7, 1973, at Newcastle City Hall, just a few miles from the Sunderland gig he had described as "the worst of my life".
Right: What's in a name? "Ziggy's", Bowie said, was the name of a tailor's shop in London, while labelmate The Legendary Stardust Cowboy contributed the surname. As a thank you, Bowie recorded the Cowboy's "I Took A Trip (On A Gemini Spaceship)" on his 2002 *Heathen* album. The image, he said, was "a cross between Nijinsky and Woolworth's."

Fantastic Voyage

While the chart positions in the US (seventy-five for the album and sixty-five for the single "Starman") never equalled those in the UK (five and ten respectively), a review in *Rolling Stone* rated *Ziggy Stardust* "at least a ninety-nine". Decades later it remains in many music fans' lists of "greatest albums ever", with every song a classic.

In 1972, of course, fans were still hunting for meaning. What was the apocalypse foretold in "Five Years"? Was "Ziggy Stardust" about Bowie himself or Jimi Hendrix? And whose "Rock 'n' Roll Suicide" were we mourning at the end?

But Bowie wasn't telling and as the Ziggy tour reached out around the world throughout 1972–73, the impact of the mythical frontman grew. And grew. And grew.

"I would never have believed in a million years that people would scream at me."

Because You're Young

Wherever the Ziggy tour went, the concert halls were packed. As each new country was added to the itinerary the venues got bigger and bigger. Nobody had ever seen anything like it. Incredible costumes designed by Yamamoto, space-age music, and a pop star who seemed to have walked off the vinyl record and straight onto the stage.

Highlights are hard to choose but three gigs at London's Rainbow Theater in August 1972 set the tone for what the rest of the world could expect. If audiences thought the sight of a band in lurex and platform shoes was weird, then the arrival of Lindsay Kemp's mime troupe onto the Finsbury Park stage saw mouths dropping open in disbelief. Most notable among the doubters, Elton John was spotted leaving early, convinced that Bowie had blown it.

Even when Kemp & Co weren't involved, Bowie's theatrical training was obvious. He didn't merely sing the songs, he acted them. One minute Ziggy was sprawled on the stage, living out his own suicide, feeling every word, the next he was trying to feel his way around an invisible brick wall in the style of Marcel Marceau. And then there was the moment when, genuflecting at Ronson's side, Ziggy performed fellatio on the guitarist's Gibson Les Paul. From the UK to the US to Japan and all over Europe the effect was the same: hysterical kids, shocked parents—and *huge* headlines.

Left and above: Ziggy's fame opened doors all over the world. In the United States legends like Stevie Wonder lined up to meet him. A few months later, on May 9, 1973, Bowie took time off from rehearsals at London's Central Studios to see Peter Cook and Dudley Moore in *Behind The Fridge* at the Cambridge Theater. Three nights later Bowie started the UK leg of the tour at Earls Court in front of 18,000 fans—a British indoor record.

"My performances have got to be theatrical experiences for me as well as for the audience."

"I refuse to be thought of as mediocre. If I am mediocre, I'll get out of the business. There's enough fog around."

The Prettiest Star

If Ziggy had been the world's introduction to a very British—if unusual —rock star, then April 1973's follow-up was where the rock star went global.

From the moment Bowie stepped off the *QE2* ship (due to his fear of flying) in New York on September 17, 1972, he knew that America had a lot to offer. Even as the first rapturous Ziggy concert got underway at the Cleveland Music Hall five days later, new ideas were forming. In fact, songwriting for the next album began in earnest the following day, with a lot of early ideas coming from Bowie's impressions of America seen from the inside of the

band's hired Greyhound bus. One new song which debuted on October 7, "The Jean Genie", began life as a mobile jam session, while "Cracked Actor" is Bowie's response to Hollywood Boulevard, and "Panic In Detroit" his account of an LA night out with Iggy Pop. Another song, "Drive-In Saturday", was composed on a train somewhere between Seattle and Phoenix.

By the time Bowie rejoined the *QE2* on December 10, most of the *Aladdin Sane* album had been written—in fact, a hurriedly recorded "Jean Genie" had already been released as a UK single, reaching number two.

Initial reactions to *Aladdin Sane* were disappointing—the album's biggest crime, it seemed, was not being *Ziggy Stardust*. In hindsight, however, this record typifies the glam rock era more than any other, from the "lightning" front cover to Mike Garson's piano frenzy on the title track and an inspired cover of The Rolling Stones' "Let's Spend The Night Together". And as the songs were added to the touring set, and Bowie's makeup and costumes became even more dramatic, fans and critics alike were in total agreement: they couldn't get enough of Aladdin Stardust.

London Bye Ta-Ta

Ziggy Stardust was already being viewed as the first "post-modern" album before the predictions of its title track came true. After eighteen months of rapidly growing global success, the third UK Ziggy tour ended with two nights at London's Hammersmith Odeon. About to launch into the last encore on the final night, Bowie said: "Of all of the shows on this tour, this particular show will remain with us the longest because not only is it the last show of the tour, but it's the last show that we'll ever do. Thank you."

As the song had foretold, now that Ziggy had made it too far, it really was time to break up the band.

Confusion shook the music world. Was it Bowie retiring, or Ziggy? And where were The Spiders?

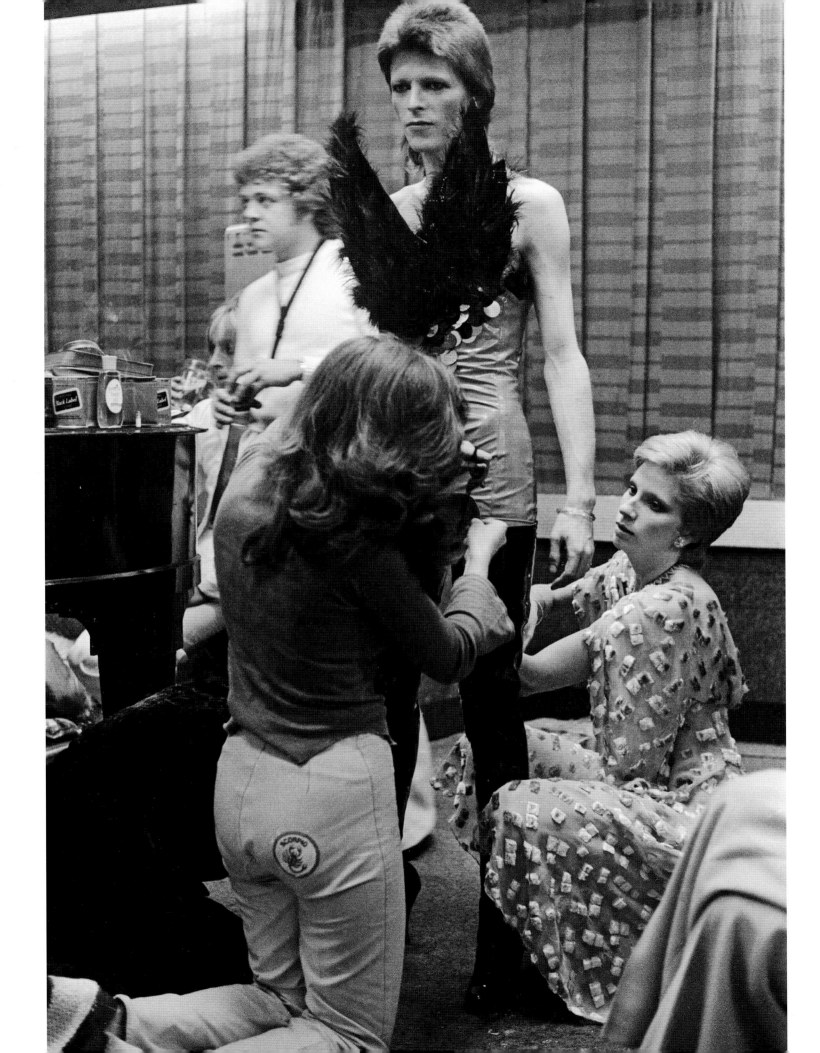

Left and above: Lesser performers might still be touring *Ziggy Stardust* now. However, Bowie, the cultural chameleon with the attention span of a five-year-old, had new clothes to try on—and they belonged to a man called Aladdin Sane. And from the reactions in New York (*left*), LA (*above with fan*), and all points in between, they seemed to fit perfectly.

Overleaf: With the arrival on tour of French makeup artist Pierre La Roche—known affectionately as Pierre La Poof—Bowie was able to let his imagination fly. La Roche (*seen center and right*) designed the silver circle for Ziggy's head and then added the iconic lightning bolt to Aladdin Sane's face decades before Harry Potter adopted a similar look.

Above: History in the making. Bowie's last night at Hammersmith Odeon, July 3, 1973, was filmed by DA Pennebaker and later released as *Ziggy Stardust: The Motion Picture*. Up until the farewell announcement just before "Rock 'n' Roll Suicide" nobody had any idea what Bowie was going to do—not even The Spiders themselves.

"I think if you're really going to entertain
an audience then you have to look the part, too."

Above: Eighteen months encapsulated in this one image from July 3, 1973, as Bowie, in his "Woodland Creatures" outfit designed by Kansai Yamamoto, performs his Marcel Marceau mime during Ronson's guitar solo.

"*Ziggy would not leave me alone for years. That was when it all started to sour.*"

Above: No other act looked like Ziggy, acted like Ziggy—nor went out like Ziggy. It was the end of an era.

Left and opposite: The Last Supper. What had been planned as an end of tour celebration at London's Café Royal became a "Retirement Party" on July 4, 1973. As David and Angie dined at the high table, guests included Paul and Linda McCartney, Keith Moon, Lulu (who had a hit with "The Man Who Sold The World" in 1974), Peter Cook and Dudley Moore, Mick and Bianca Jagger (*below between David and Angie*), Jeff Beck, Tony Curtis, and Lou Reed.

Left: The marriage of Angie and David was publicly "open" from the start. Both had lovers, some of whom lived with them at Haddon Hall and stayed when they moved to Chelsea. David's rumored romance with backup singer Ava Cherry saw him write songs for her as part of The Astronettes.
Right: It was Angie who encouraged Bowie to dress as Ziggy even when not on stage. Although the character had retired, the flamboyant hairstyle remained.

Move On

1973 was the year of David Bowie. Apart from dominating world headlines and setting attendance records wherever he toured, by July all five of his albums were in the UK Top Forty—and *Aladdin Sane* was at number one. He even scored two top ten singles—although the first was against his wishes.

Having watched his career take off, Bowie's first label, Deram, decided to capitalize. On September 8, 1973, much to Bowie's embarrassment, they released "The Laughing Gnome". Constant radio play meant it soon reached number six.

A month later he was relieved to see "Sorrow", from his new album of 1960s covers, *Pin Ups*, make number three in the UK. Recorded in France in July, this collection of old Who, Pretty Things, and Easybeats numbers was little more than Bowie's hurried reply to RCA's demands for another album. New material, however, was just around the corner—and it was his darkest yet.

Above: Bowie leaves Victoria Station, and his wife, to travel to Paris to record *Pin Ups* at the Château d'Hérouville studios, July 9, 1973.
Opposite: The Ziggy look lived on, even if the character did not.

Left: Ziggy is dead, long live Bowie. On October 18–21, 1973, fan club members were invited to London's Marquee Club to see Bowie's latest assault on the American market. Called *The 1980 Floor Show* (the pun indicating Bowie's next project), the event comprised a performance of ten songs filmed for the US *Midnight Special* TV program, including a duet with Marianne Faithfull, in a nun's habit, on "I Got You Babe".

Opposite and below left: A couple of nods to the Ziggy era included his "angel of death" costume and the final appearance of Mick Ronson and Trevor Bolder in Bowie's band, alongside members of new group The Astronettes.

Left: Despite a front cover featuring Bowie and young model Twiggy in Aladdin Sane-style makeup, the *Pin Ups* record itself was 1960s rock 'n' roll, pure and simple. It was also the fourth and last album to be produced by Ken Scott, the man Bowie described as "my George Martin".

Overleaf left: Bowie and friend in another of the images rejected by RCA for the cover of *Diamond Dogs*. **Overleaf right:** Signing fans' hands, clothes, and anything else they can produce.

"I thought Ziggy was a beautiful piece of art, I really did. I thought it was a grand kitsch painting. The whole guy."

Growin' Up

The clue to Bowie's next project had already been given in the title to his *Midnight Special* ("1980 Floor"). New songs premiered on the show—"Dodo" and "1984"—weren't from a new album, however. They were from a musical Bowie was writing.

About George Orwell's *1984*!

At least that had been the plan. When Orwell's widow refused to hand over stage rights Bowie fell to Plan B: he would just have to create his own future dystopia instead. Hunger City was born.

Diamond Dogs, released in April 1974, saw Ziggy Stardust replaced with his near-identical twin Halloween Jack. There was certainly a familiar "Stardust" feel to songs like "Rebel Rebel" and the title track, despite only part-time Spider Mike Garson appearing on the recordings, but there was also a hint at a completely new direction.

Lyrically, Bowie's new influence was the author William Burroughs, whose fragmentary style of writing—literally throwing passages into the air and seeing how they fell—was adopted on many of the tracks. Musically, however, with the "wah-wah" guitar sounds on "1984" and melodies on "Rock 'n' Roll With Me" leading the way, this was very much a jump in the direction of funky American soul.

And then there was the cover. Only a few of the original version featuring a painting of Bowie's torso on a dog's reclining body escaped into public hands before RCA noticed the creature's gender was anatomically correct in a very graphic way. Different replacement sleeves were quickly issued.

Despite very little in the way of promotion, *Diamond Dogs* gave Bowie his third UK number one in a row and his first *Billboard* top ten placing.

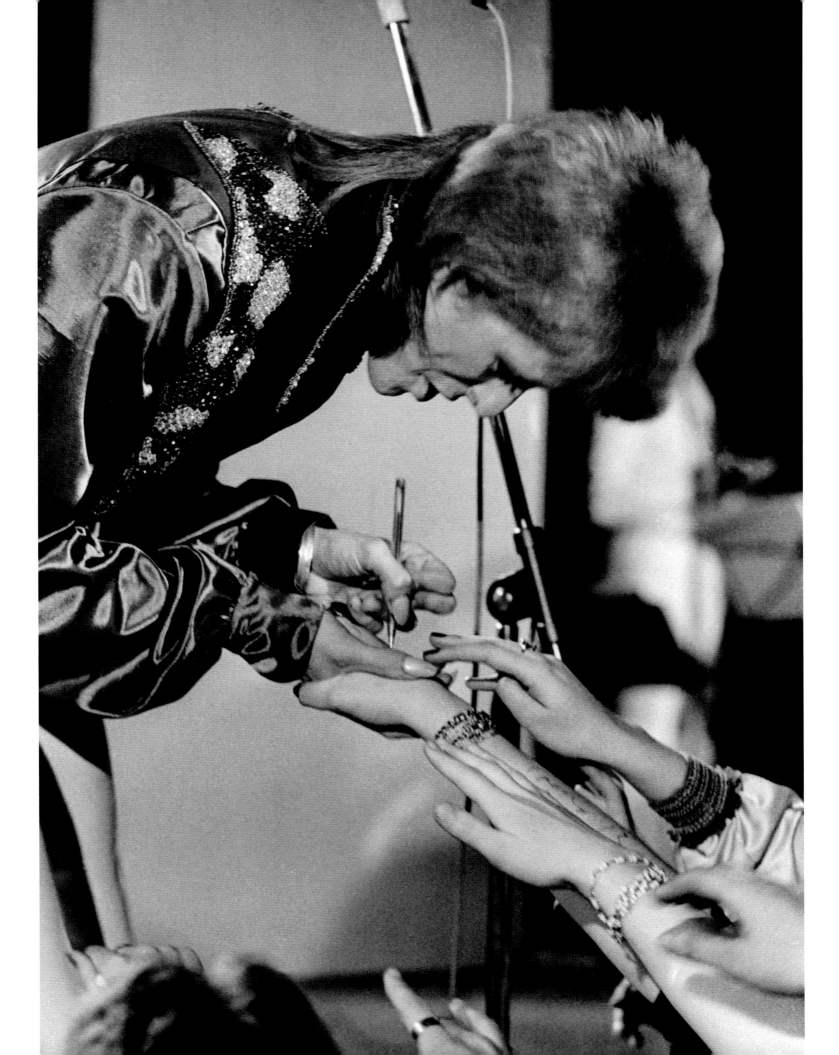

Left: Full Ziggy hair, cigarette, and pirate patch for Bowie's press conference at the Amstel Hotel, Amsterdam, on February 13, 1974.
Right: Performing "Rebel Rebel" in the Top Pop Studios, Hilversum, on February 13, 1974. The song's single release, although a regular concert favorite ever since, marked the end of Bowie's affair with glam rock.

Without You

Part of *Diamond Dogs* was recorded at The Netherlands' Ludolf Studios in Hilversum, so it was only appropriate that Bowie should return there in February 1974 to pick up an award for *Ziggy Stardust*. In a room full of black-ties and white-noise, he strolled in with his red hair at full mast and sporting a pirate's eye-patch (supposedly as a result of conjunctivitis). Halloween Jack really was a real cool cat.

As he took his bows, how many of the audience realized that this would be the last public appearance of the "Ziggy Look"? Did Bowie himself even know?

Of course he did. Glam rock had launched on his tails and now it would die in his wake. He was going home to change his clothes, to change his hair. To change himself. *Again.*

Chapter 3

He Was a Young American

Above: After a four-album absence, Tony Visconti was called back in to mix *Diamond Dogs*, which Bowie had produced himself. Unlike the last time they had worked together, on *The Man Who Sold The World*, Bowie was focused and in control. The cocaine in his bag, he said, was for purely social use. It wouldn't be long until his priorities began to change.

Opposite: The chameleon at work. David Bowie, unrecognizable from the kabuki-dressed glam-rocker of 1973.

Previous page: David Bowie, 1974, at the cutting-edge of fashion and music.

Left: There were no doubts where MainMan's priorities for Bowie lay. The big audiences, and the big money, were in the United States.

Left below and right: The Diamond Dogs tour, which began at the Montreal Forum on June 14, 1974, was Bowie's most elaborate yet. By the time the show reached Minnesota in October it had evolved into the Philly Dogs tour.

This is Not America

While Ziggy Stardust had made Bowie a household name in the UK, in the most important market in the world—the USA—he was still relatively unknown. It was a situation his management company, MainMan, and boss Tony Defries in particular, could not allow to continue. And so, in April 1974, Bowie packed his bags once again for New York.

Leaving Angie at home to raise Zowie and pursue their old hedonistic lifestyle, Bowie surrounded himself with a new team. MainMan staffer Corinne "Coco" Schwab became his personal assistant, his "Halloween Jack" persona transformed into a baggy-suited, fedora-sporting "gouster" look and a marked side-parting wrangled control of his still orange hair. The chameleon's biggest change, however, was chemical. His best friend right now was cocaine.

Left: The US Halloween Jack was a more sober version than that seen in Europe. Long collar shirts and baggy pants replaced the eye-patch and red play suits.
Above: Like so many Americans, David Cassidy's younger brother and future Hardy Boy, Shaun, couldn't wait to meet Bowie.

" My problem was cocaine, and then I went from cocaine to alcohol, which is a natural course of events."

"1984"

The Diamond Dogs tour was the most extravagant concert series ever undertaken. Whether sitting backwards on a chair, à la Liza Minnelli, suspended by an invisible crane while singing into a telephone for "Space Oddity", or sporting suspenders and boxing gloves, Bowie the Actor threw himself into every song. Most of the set came from *Diamond Dogs* and *Aladdin Sane* but where was the band? Years before Pink Floyd hid from audiences in *The Wall*, here were Earl Slick—handling all Mick Ronson's solos with aplomb—Herbie Flowers on bass, plus oboe, flute, percussion, sax players, and backup singers all being made to perform unseen by the paying crowd. It was radical, it was theatrical, and it was ultimately unsustainable.

Above and opposite: A week before *Young Americans* was released, featuring the US number one single, "Fame", a pale and gaunt Bowie joined collaborator John Lennon, his wife Yoko Ono, Paul Simon, and Art Garfunkel at NYC's Uris Theater for the seventeenth Grammy Awards, March 1, 1975. A combination of hard work and hard drugs seemed to be taking a physical toll.

Stateside

The album *David Live* must have seemed a good idea at the time but it barely captures the majesty of that 1974 extravaganza. Bowie seems out of sorts vocally and we now know that the band were unhappy at performing out of sight each night. But for anyone lucky enough to see the shows it serves as an unforgettable aural postcard.

Bowie himself has dismissed the record as "David Bowie Is Alive And Well And Living Only In Theory" and there is some truth in the wordplay. Cocaine had suddenly become a very important part of his life. His wife Angie's later claim that

he had moved to NYC to be closer to his drug dealer is probably wide of the mark—he was a social user when he arrived. But the role of substance abuser was just another in which he could become totally immersed. His visibly plummeting weight, gaunt features, and paranoid, twitching behavior during a BBC documentary filmed during the tour, *Cracked Actor*, all pointed to a habit out of control.

But work continued. During a summer break Bowie took members of the touring band into a Philadelphia studio to work on new sounds. When

the second phase of the tour kicked off in Los Angeles on September 2, 1974, he realized that not only was the Hunger City stage set an ill fit for his new musical direction, but it was simply too expensive. As a result, the third leg, beginning a month later in Minnesota, saw all the theatrical trappings pared back and a new name assigned to incorporate the latest material: the Philly Dogs tour. Joining him onstage now was a new line-up including young guitarist Carlos Alomar and five backup singers, among them Ava Cherry and a young man called Luther Vandross.

Win

The stage show and personnel were not the only clues to a change of direction. Of the four new songs premiered in the fall shows, three of them displayed just why Bowie had surrounded himself with the cream of young, black talent. "Win", "Somebody Up There Likes Me", and "Can You Hear Me" were as soulful as 1971's "She Shook Me Cold" was heavy rock. Even a fourth newcomer, the infectious "Young Americans", had strong Latin rhythms. By the time Bowie's album of the same name was released in March 1975, the radical shift from glam rock was no surprise to concert-goers. Taking over where the funk of "1984" had left off, the new songs were, Bowie said self-deprecatingly, his attempts at "plastic soul". While the UK shook its head in despair, the US lapped it up, with lead single, "Fame", a collaboration with Alomar and John Lennon, becoming Bowie's first US number one. The gamble to relocate had paid off.

Opposite: Playing sax with Keith Moon at Peter Sellers' fiftieth birthday party in LA, September 1, 1975.
Left: With Ronnie Wood and Bill Wyman at Peter Sellers' birthday celebrations.
Overleaf: As filming on *The Man Who Fell to Earth* is planned, leading man Bowie embraces fellow actor Elizabeth Taylor in Beverly Hills, 1975.

"Living in Los Angeles is like being trapped in the set of a movie you didn't want to see in the first place."

Opposite top: Director Nic Roeg in discussion with his star, summer 1975. Bowie was perfectly cast as the alien sent to Earth to exploit its water resources for his own planet's survival. If anything, Bowie says, Roeg exploited his disconnected state of mind to get a better performance.
Opposite and left: On the set of his first feature film, *The Man Who Fell to Earth*. In several shots he is wearing the hood that would appear on the album cover of *Low*.
Left bottom: The same room used for the cover shot of *Station To Station*.

Loving the Alien

Thomas Jerome Newton looked like David Bowie from the *Young Americans* era, maybe more ashen and neat, perhaps just a bit more distant than usual. But there was something else about him. He was an alien. And he had fallen to Earth.

Bowie's acting career had begun and largely ended in the 1960s with a series of short films (released years later as *Love You Till Tuesday*). But in 1975 when director Nic Roeg was casting for someone to play his disconnected, otherly-looking intergalactic visitor, he thought of Bowie. So many familiar themes came suddenly together: starmen, the apocalypse, relationships and the future, all packaged in sumptuous colors and elaborate sets. It could have been written for him.

Other films would follow, but *The Man Who Fell to Earth* would remain Bowie's finest celluloid moment.

Station to Station

Despite weighing as little as ninety-eight pounds and existing on a diet of red and green peppers, in 1975 Bowie not only managed to film his first major movie, but also record a new album. For once he did not have to look far for a character. He was actually living the life of The Thin White Duke.

Home for the increasingly paranoid singer was an Egyptian-influenced property in Hollywood, where his addictions and interests in the mythical could co-exist. His life was almost totally distinct from Angie's now—as, in fact, it seemed to be from reality itself.

When the new material was released in January 1976, after Bowie had promised, "I have rocked my last roll," nobody had any reason to expect just how good it would be. But *Station To Station* was brilliant. The soul influences remained but there was a darker heart and an emotional distance that was pure European. The title track, "Golden Years" and "Word On A Wing" remain classics today.

There was a flip-side to The Thin White Duke, however, and Bowie's public utterances became more explosive. Saying that "Britain could

benefit from a Fascist leader" after "Hitler was the first pop star" did not go down well. Ironically, asked to give up booked satellite time following the death of the Spanish dictator, Franco, Bowie refused, instead speaking by satellite to UK TV's Russell Harty about his forthcoming Isolar tour. "I'm coming home in May to play shows, look at you and be English again," he promised. When Bowie did arrive at London's Victoria Station on May 2, and was photographed, some said, giving a "sieg heil" salute, it was a controversy that went too far.

Previous pages left: Bowie denies giving a "sieg heil" salute at London's Victoria Station, May 2, 1976. "Not even I was capable of that." The "swastika" imagery in "China Girl", however, indicated an interest in the subject.

Previous pages right: The Isolar tour—otherwise known as Station To Station, The Thin White Duke, and White Light—reaches Denmark's Falkoner Teatret, April 29. The tour ran from February 2 to May 18, 1976, taking in the United States, Canada and, for the first time in three years, Europe.

Above: Bowie and Dutch transsexual actor Romy Haag at the L'Alcazar Club, Paris, celebrating the final night of the Isolar tour, May 18, 1976.

Opposite: By the time he was joined by Monique van Vooren at the premiere of *Close Encounters Of The Third Kind* at the Ziegfeld Theater, New York, November 15, 1977, Bowie's marriage to Angie was over in all but name.

Join the Gang

Not only did Bowie finish, against the odds, his 1976 tour, but also he did so in style. Stepping off the stage in Paris on May 18 he was, if anything, reinvigorated —and ready to reinvent. His first decision was to put some distance between himself and the temptations of Hollywood. For tax purposes Bowie and entourage relocated officially to Switzerland and Angie and Zowie moved in too. It was time to get clean and play happy families once more.

Work, however, took place across the border at France's Château d'Hérouville, where *Pin Ups* had been recorded. It

was here that Iggy Pop's *The Idiot* was recorded in a burst of feverish collaboration, and the beginnings of a fresh project, *Low*. Both albums wouldn't be finished, however, until Bowie had moved once again, this time to Berlin, home of his latest obsession: Kraut-rock.

Despite his intentions, Bowie's life was still dictated by his addictions. Half of every week was lost to either taking drugs or their comedown—but the amount he achieved in the other half would put modern musicians to shame. A second Iggy Pop album, *Lust For Life,* was written, recorded, and produced in

eight days. So strong was their creative relationship that Bowie even joined Pop's touring band as pianist.

But it was the collaborations on his own work that really bore fruit. Tony Visconti returned as producer. However, it was the influence of Brian Eno, former bit-part player with glam rockers Roxy Music, that shaped *Low*. He persuaded Bowie to take risks, to experiment, to be brave. Which is why, to RCA's horror, the finished album contained a whole side of extended instrumentals. At a time when the world was discovering punk, what was Bowie doing?

Above: David Bowie on backup vocals and keyboards as part of Iggy Pop's twenty-nine-date Idiot tour, California, 1977.
Opposite left: Tourmates Bowie and Iggy board the train at Denmark's Copenhagen station, January 23, 1977.
Opposite right: At a station in Germany, 1977. Bowie later released his own versions of the duo's "China Girl", "Neighborhood Threat", "Tonight", and "Sister Midnight" (the last as "Red Money").

"The first side of Low was all about me, but side two was more an observation in musical terms of my reaction to seeing the East bloc."

Left: Nobody saw this one coming. Bowie's appearance alongside Bing Crosby for a duet of "Peace On Earth/Little Drummer Boy" in summer 1977 was recorded two days before he sang "Heroes" next to Marc Bolan on his old friend's show, *Marc*. In both cases, it was the last show each collaborator would do.
Right: The iconic cover image for *Heroes*, the second of Bowie's Berlin Trilogy.

A Small Plot of Land

If the sound of *Young Americans* had been shaped by being recorded mostly in Philadelphia, then Bowie's decision to create *Heroes* in a studio directly overlooking the Berlin Wall had to influence his work there. Taking the look of their surroundings, after all, is exactly how chameleons work.

It wasn't just the titles of two of the four new instrumentals—"V-2 Schneider" and "Neuköln"—that sounded teutonic. The Turkish feel of "Neuköln" reflected Berlin's immigrant culture, "Blackout" the city's nightlife, while the lovers meeting by the Wall in

"Heroes" could only have been referring to one specific place. Once again, Bowie, Visconti, and Eno, with discordant guitar courtesy Robert Fripp, delivered a record completely unexpected. "Joe The Lion" and "Beauty And The Beast" once again employed the Burroughs cut'n'see approach, and the whole album seemed an angrier attempt to shock next to the synth-led reflection of *Low*.

Released in October 1977, *Heroes* concluded a year of abundant studio activity. Bowie was happier, healthier, and more alive than any time since 1973. It was time to get back on the road.

PAUL DAINTY PRESENTS

David Bowie

LIVE ON STAGE

WITH SPECIAL GUESTS THE ANGELS

SYDNEY SHOWGROUND
FRIDAY, 24th NOVEMBER, 1978
at 7.30 p.m.

Please retain ticket (Subject to conditions on back of ticket)

WE PLAY RAIN OR SHINE

Nº 23237

PAUL DAINTY PRESENTS

David Bowie

LIVE ON STAGE

SYDNEY SHOWGROUND

FRIDAY, 24th NOVEMBER, 1978, 7.30 p.m.

Nº 23237

Stay

As the 1970s drew to a close, no man had made a bigger cultural impact than David Bowie. By visiting Australia during 1978's Isolar II tour he had performed in every major western city. He even managed to find time mid-tour to record the final part of his Berlin Trilogy.

Released in May 1979, *Lodger* was a more straightforward album than its predecessors. Strong narrative songs like "Look Back In Anger" and "Repetition" stand out, and there are no instrumentals. However, the bold instinct was still there. "Boys Keep Swinging" was captured by band members swapping their instruments while subjects such as the holocaust and domestic abuse feature lyrically.

It was in this serious frame of mind that Bowie began steps to separate legally from Angie. He didn't care about the financial settlement or any terms.

He just wanted his son Zowie.

Opposite: Bowie's relationship with Angie is thought to have broken down irrevocably after Christmas, 1977. It was part in readiness for a custody battle over Zowie that he, with Iggy Pop, tried a self-imposed attempt at kicking his addictions.

Above: At Earls Court, London, June 29, 1978.

Right: Costumes for the 1978 tour were designed by Natasha Korniloff from his days with Lindsay Kemp (she would later provide his Pierrot clown's outfit for "Ashes to Ashes"). On the other hand, Bowie's "geography teacher" chic offstage was entirely his own choice.

Left: Appearing variously as an oriental air stewardess, wrapped in a cardboard coat, and dancing as though a marionette, Bowie's performance of "The Man Who Sold The World", "Boys Keep Swinging", and "TVC15" for *Saturday Night Live* saw his troupe augmented by Blondie's Jimmy Destri and performance artists Klaus Nomi and Joey Arias, pictured here. December 16, 1979.

Right: They were once his closest rivals for glam rock's crown, but an Eno-less Roxy Music thrilled Bowie enough to catch them at Philadelphia's Tower Theater, March 30, 1979, and to later record Bryan Ferry's "If There Is Something" with Tin Machine.

Right: One project to come out of Bowie's Berlin years was not a record. David Hemmings' *Just A Gigolo* was filmed in the city in spring 1978 and starred Bowie alongside Sydney Rome—seen here promoting the movie on February 15, 1979—and Marlene Dietrich. After the acclaim of his leading man debut, this was a disaster. "Imagine how we felt," Bowie says. "It was my thirty-two Elvis Presley movies rolled into one!"

Chapter 4

The Serious Moonlight

Above and right: Having conquered celluloid with *The Man Who Fell To Earth*, Bowie leapt at the chance to play John Merrick in the Broadway production of *The Elephant Man*. He and co-star Patricia Elliott are congratulated by Gilda Radner, on opening night, September 28, 1980; arriving at the theater.

Opposite: Still in makeup, a relieved Bowie enjoys the response that his mime-influenced performance received in front of its first audience.

Previous page: David Bowie, superstar, in Rotterdam's Feyenoord Stadium, June 25, 1983.

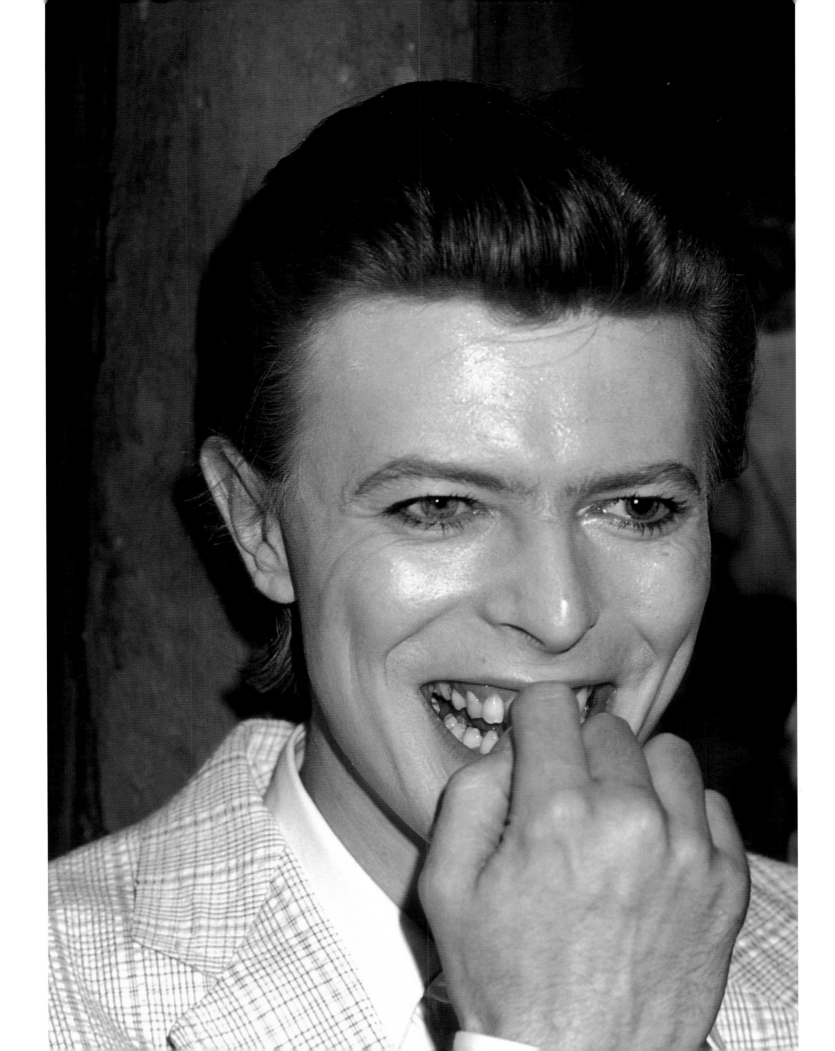

Right: Bowie was an international star but he was still relevant to punk rockers. In fact, sharing a drink with Paul Simonon, bassist with The Clash, following the band's night at Shea Stadium, October 12, 1982, Bowie was about to become bigger than he had ever been before.

Five Years

At the start of the new decade, Bowie could do no wrong. On a personal level his divorce from Angie was finally completed in March 1980, with the courts awarding him custody of their son, now called "Joe". And musically he was on fire.

Released in September 1980, *Scary Monsters (And Super Creeps)* was Bowie's strongest work for years—arguably his best ever. No longer shackled by Eno's adventurism, he and Visconti created a visceral soundscape of emotional chaos wrapped in masterful guitar work from Robert Fripp and extraordinary songwriting. "Ashes To Ashes" completed the story of Major Tom, also topping the UK charts;

"Fashion" won a new wave of followers, while the title track and "It's No Game" showed the true possibilities of punk. (He reached number one in the UK again in 1981 with "Under Pressure", a collaboration with rock group Queen that had evolved when they recorded in Montreux, near his Swiss home, and he happened to drop by.)

Unexpectedly, Bowie decided not to tour in support of *Scary Monsters*, opting instead to play the lead in *The Elephant Man* on Broadway. But inspired by his chart resurrection, work began with Nile Rodgers on new songs in late 1982. Bowie's next tour would be the globe-trotting Serious Moonlight. And the album would be called *Let's Dance*.

Above: In 1983 Bowie became a genuine superstar. His first album in a $17 million deal with EMI America, *Let's Dance*, was his biggest selling ever. The title track hit number one on both sides of the Atlantic and the Serious Moonlight tour was about to take him to more people than ever before.

Above right: A decade later, some of the theatricality of the Diamond Dogs shows was back. Wembley Arena, June 2, 1983.

Above: The whole band, including Slick and Alomar again, plus Carmine Rojas, Tony Thompson, Dave Lebolt, Steve Elson, Stan Harrison, Lenny Pickett, and brothers George and Frank Simms, wore *Our Man In Havana* styling.

Above right: New fans had come for hits like "China Girl", "Modern Love", "Let's Dance", and "Cat People", but 1983 was also the first chance to hear *Lodger*'s "Look Back In Anger" and "Red Sails" and *Scary Monster*'s "Ashes To Ashes", "Fashion", and "Scary Monsters" itself performed live.

"I was always quite happy with the amount that I sold up until Let's Dance, but when that happened I was delighted to say the least."

Left: From Brussels on May 18 to Hong Kong on December 8, the Serious Moonlight tour sold 2,601,196 tickets for ninety-six dates in sixteen countries. At the Auteuil's Hippodrome in Paris, June 9 (*top*); Milton Keynes, England, July 1(*bottom*).

Above: The two biggest stars in the world. After a decade of success Bowie is congratulated backstage by Michael Jackson, eight months after the release of *Thriller*. Bette Midler, Timothy Hutton, and Cher look on.

Right: Just another day in the life of a legend.

Previous pages: The trappings of
success. On September 13, 1983, Bowie
arrived at London's Madame Tussauds to
be measured and matched for his
waxwork (*left*). Meanwhile, former
manager Ken Pitt displays the boots from
the "Space Oddity" video at a Bowie
convention, October 1; while a UK Bowie
fan shows the extent of his fascination.
Left: As Status Quo take to the stage at
Wembley Stadium to begin Live Aid,
Bowie shares a joke with Queen's Roger
Taylor and Brian May. In front of them, the
Prince and Princess of Wales and organizer
Bob Geldof, July 13, 1985.

No Control

Everything Bowie touched in 1983
seemed to work. New roles that year in
vampire flick *The Hunger* and prisoner-
of-war story *Merry Christmas, Mr.
Lawrence*, won critical plaudits,
encouraging a new enthusiasm for
acting. The films *Labyrinth*, *Absolute
Beginners*, *The Last Temptation Of Christ*,
Yellowbeard, and *Into The Night* all
followed in the 1980s, with varying
degrees of success.

There was a downturn, however, in
fortunes with the release of his next
album in 1984. Whereas *Let's Dance*
had energized the world with its clean
pop sound, *Tonight* seemed thrown
together. Tellingly, of the album's nine
tracks, only two—the singles "Blue Jean"
and "Loving The Alien"—were written
by Bowie alone. It still reached number
eleven in the US and one in the UK, but
for many fans the magic was missing.

Opposite: For Geldof's "Global Jukebox" idea to work he needed legends—and in 1985 they didn't come bigger than Bowie.

Left: Coming on to the surprising "TVC15", Bowie then wowed the crowd with "Rebel Rebel" and "Modern Love" before an emotional "Heroes", dedicated to "my son, to all our children, and to the children of the world."

Left middle: As Paul McCartney's microphone problems threatened to ruin the former Beatle's rendition of "Let It Be", Bowie joined Alison Moyet, The Who's Pete Townshend, and Bob Geldof as impromptu backup singers.

Left bottom: The original plan had been to attempt a live transatlantic duet, but satellite delays meant that only the video was shown of Bowie's collaboration with Mick Jagger on "Dancing In The Street". The song reached number seven on the *Billboard* chart and top spot in the UK, raising more money for the famine relief effort.

Heroes

Bowie may have been accused of "selling out" on his recent recordings, but in 1985 there was no better man to call if you wanted to stage the biggest concert in history. Bob Geldof's campaign to "Feed The World" had already topped the transatlantic charts, but after booking Philadelphia's JFK Stadium and Wembley in London, now he needed legendary names to fill the stage. And Bowie was one of the first people he called.

Geldof wasn't disappointed. Not only was Bowie's performance one of the highlights of Live Aid, but he was also chosen to introduce important footage from Ethiopia and, with Pete Townshend and Alison Moyet, joined Geldof alongside Paul McCartney to end the London side of the "global jukebox".

Above: Elder statesmen of rock, Mick Jagger and David Bowie, duet with an all-star band including Paul McCartney, Mark Knopfler, Mark King, and Bryan Adams, at the Prince's Trust Concert, Wembley Arena, June 23, 1986.

Opposite: Bowie's turn as Jareth the Goblin King in Jim Henson's *Labyrinth* has become a cult classic. Bowie also recorded several new songs for the soundtrack.

"Every time I make an album,
I tend to take the road
to commercial suicide."

Never Get Old

Myriad film projects piqued Bowie's interest after Live Aid. A duet with Pat Metheny on the *Falcon And The Snowman* soundtrack led to the hit "This Is Not America", while new songs from *Absolute Beginners*, *Labyrinth,* and *When The Wind Blows* also charted. But where was he going to go next? After the incredible success of *Scary Monsters* and *Let's Dance*, on both of which Bowie had noticeably retaken control of his music, *Tonight* was seen as a backwards step. It was an album by committee once again. If Bowie had a character now, what was it?

And more importantly, *where* was it? On the face of it, April 1987's *Never Let Me Down* seemed to tick all the required boxes. Eight of the eleven tracks are solo compositions and there was no doubting Bowie's energy during promotional interviews. But critical response was scathing and it became his least successful album in a decade. The album's token Iggy Pop covers—traditionally included, Iggy has hinted, to keep him in royalties—were weak and some of the originals seemed almost out of date. Was David Bowie in danger of becoming irrelevant?

Opposite top: Bowie and Jagger—two acts whose hits may have dried up since the late 1980s, but whose ability to fill football stadia all over the world has only been increased.

Opposite bottom: A lean, focused Bowie prepares for his biggest tour yet, the theatrical behemoth that is The Glass Spider, 1987.

Above: Back in his former home town of Berlin, against the Wall that inspired "Heroes".

Left: Rehearsing in NYC. As usual, Bowie wanted two guitarists on tour. Joining Carlos Alomar on six-string duties for *Never Let Me Down* and the Glass Spider spectacular was Peter Frampton (*far right*), whose father had taught Bowie art in Bromley many years earlier, and whose band Humble Pie Bowie had supported back in 1969.

Look Back in Anger

Encouraged by terrible reviews, even Bowie himself admits *Never Let Me Down* was a mistake. But the three million fans who packed out venues like Giants Stadium all over the globe on the Glass Spider tour seemed to disagree. This was his grandest, most theatrical production yet. There were dancers, athletes, and madmen swarming the stage. Lines were learned, parts were played, and actors flew over every inch of the *Mad Max*-themed set. Left, right, up and down. And Bowie—dangling by a rope one minute, leading a six-person mime sequence the next in homage once again to Lindsay Kemp, all while sporting immaculate suits and unfeasible coiffed hair—was involved in it all. It was spectacular, bold, and the last time he would ever do something on this scale.

After six exhausting months Bowie was drained. Commercially and critically he was at a crossroads. As the 1980s neared their end, could the chameleon reinvent himself one more time?

"It was so great to burn the spider in New Zealand at the end of the tour. We just put the thing in a field and set light to it."

Left: The Glass Spider, Bowie said, was his attempt to get back to the audacity of the Diamond Dogs tour which only parts of the United States had seen. He even reintroduced that tour's singing into a telephone while suspended fifty feet above the stage, this time for "The Glass Spider".
Above: The angel Bowie resurrected and in control. Eighty-six exhausting dates from Rotterdam on May 30, 1987 to New Zealand on November 28.

Chapter 5

Modern Life

Above: In performance art mode with Louise Lecavalier from Canadian dance troupe La La La Human Steps. The duo's interpretation of "Look Back In Anger" for the Institute of Contemporary Arts in London revitalized Bowie's expressive powers in July 1988.
Opposite: The stunning choreography and multi-media presentation was a key part of the international TV special *Wrap Around The World*, in September 1988.
Previous page: Honored with a star on the Hollywood Walk of Fame, February 12, 1997.

"There was too much responsibility on the last tour. It was a decision a second."

Art Decade

The fact that the Glass Spider extravaganza was Bowie's attempt to recreate the Diamond Dogs tour was the first real indication that the great originator, the man who had inspired a generation of copycat artists, had begun to run out of new ideas. 1988, in fact, became the first year since 1971 that he had not had a UK top forty single. Stung by the critical reaction to his recent work, Bowie responded in the only way he knew how.

By tearing up the rule book.

Bowie's performance of "Look Back In Anger" at London's "Intruder In The Palace" arts event was exceptional. A nine-minute, delete hard rock reworking of the song was only half the story, however. As Bowie and dancer Louise Lecavalier prowled every inch of the stage stroking, throwing, and hitting each other, pre-recorded scenes of similar passion were intercut on large screens. Bowie the Performance Artist was born.

Credit for the hard-edged reworking of the old *Lodger* song, however, went to guitarist Reeves Gabrels who, along with *Lust For Life*'s rhythm section, Hunt and Tony Sales, would form Bowie's next project: Tin Machine.

Above: Bowie as a member of a band for the first time since the 1960s. Brixton Academy, London, November 11, 1991.
Right: The members of Tin Machine rehearse at Manhattan Center Studios in New York City, May 25, 1989. (*left to right*) Tony Sales, David Bowie, Hunt Sales, and Reeves Gabrels.

"Tin Machine was Reeves Gabrels shaking me out of my doldrums, pointing me at some kind of light, saying: be adventurous again!"

Sound and Vision

He wanted to do anything, it seems, other than be David Bowie—Pop Star. Rumor has it, in fact, that without Tin Machine he might have quit music altogether and gone back to his painting. For the first time, probably since the early days with Ken Pitt or Angie, Bowie felt able to share responsibility for his decisions with others. If audiences didn't like the music then it wasn't just him shouldering the fall-out. As it turned out, the first Tin Machine album was well received. Fans even liked Bowie's beard. The second, however, was less successful and the live album, *Oy Vey, Baby*, released in 1992, failed to chart in the UK or US.

Tin Machine wasn't Bowie's only attempt to start again. In 1990, in between group projects, he embarked on his Sound + Vision tour, which, he promised, would be the last time he played all his early hits. Luckily, fans in twenty-seven countries had 108 concerts in which to catch "Life On Mars?" and "Space Oddity" before their retirement. Insisting once again that his band perform largely from behind multi-media screens, Bowie rediscovered his taste for being center of attention.

Bowie was back!

Above: Bowie never forgot his roots, turning up to launch the Brixton community center, yards from where he was born in Stanfield Road, having donated £200,000 to get the project off the ground. July 6, 1989.
Opposite: Bowie the artist and art connoisseur in London (*top*) and with one of his own works at the Eduard Nakhamkin Fine Arts Gallery in New York City, November 27, 1990.

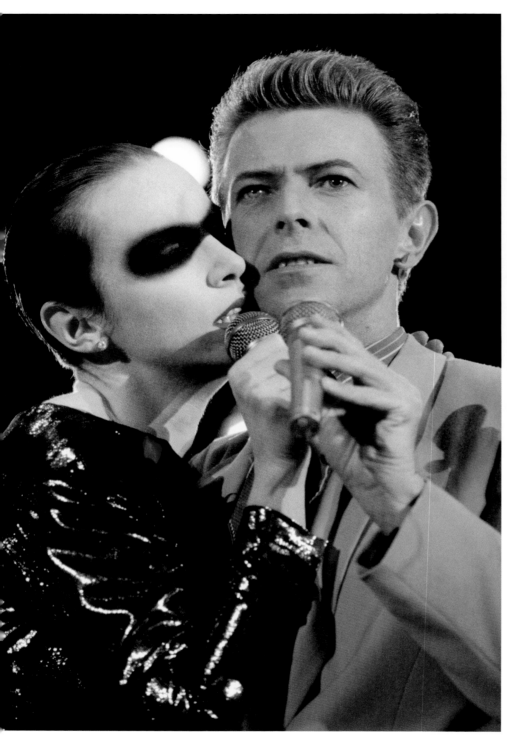

Left: Performing "Under Pressure" with Annie Lennox at the Freddie Mercury Tribute Concert, Wembley Stadium, April 20, 1992. The death of Queen's Freddie Mercury in 1991 was the highest profile AIDS-related loss so far. When Bowie later dedicated the Lord's Prayer to all sufferers, it was a gesture that made headlines around the world.

Above: It was fantastic enough seeing Mick Ronson on guitar for "Heroes", but when Ian Hunter arrived for "All The Young Dudes" and Bowie picked up his sax, 72,000 people went mad.

"I idolized John Coltrane and Eric Dolphy, and learned to play the clarinet and tenor saxophone when I was twelve. When I first came into the business it was as a jazz musician."

Opposite top: Four days after reciting *that* prayer on a TV show broadcast live to millions of viewers around the globe, Bowie was in more private mode when he married his girlfriend, Iman Abdulmajid, at a small ceremony in Lausanne, Switzerland. He had met the Somalian supermodel at a party on October 14, 1990, following the break-up of his relationship with Glass Spider dancer Melissa Hurley.

Opposite bottom and left: To promote his 1995 album *Outside* Bowie decided to try something new. Fans who lined up for a signature at his first ever in-store appearance weren't complaining. HMV, NYC, September 26, 1995.

"I tend to steal from high art and demean it to street level."

Left: Bowie-as-Warhol on the set of *Basquiat*, New York, June 5, 1995, his first film since *The Linguini Incident* and *Twin Peaks: Fire Walk With Me*, released four years earlier. Of his later roles, playing himself in *Zoolander* in 2001 and Nicola Tesla in 2006's *The Prestige* rank highest critically.

Right: The King of Cool meets the Prime Minister of "Cool Britannia" as Bowie is handed an award for Outstanding Contribution by Tony Blair at the Brit Awards, February 19, 1996, and gives the shortest speech of the night: "Thank you, Tony, thank you everyone else. I think I'll go and sing at you."

"Playing Warhol was great. I only had 7,000 words, and once I got them in the right order, it was a doddle."

Wishful Beginnings

Bowie's Lausanne marriage to Iman had been a private affair but the later blessing in Florence was a very public declaration of his love. The celebrity magazine *Hello!* captured pictures of best man Duncan Jones, as Zowie/Joe was now called, smiling alongside the oddly named triumvirate Brian Eno, Yoko Ono, and Bono, and even the wedding music, composed by Bowie himself, was released on his next studio album. In fact, the whole of *Black Tie White Noise* was conceived as little more than the singer's open love letter to his new wife.

While Iman would never see her husband achieve the commercial heights that his first wife witnessed—although his reputation and influence would never be greater—she certainly inspired new levels of creativity. In the same year as *Black Tie White Noise* Bowie also recorded a full soundtrack album for the Hanif Kureishi drama *The Buddha Of Suburbia*. Then, in 1995, not only did the first gallery exhibition of Bowie's own paintings take place, but also he adopted a gray mop wig for a convincing turn as Andy Warhol in the film *Basquiat,* and even created a new genre—the "non-linear gothic drama hyper cycle"—for

his new album, *1.Outside*. As Nile Rodgers had returned last time, so Eno came back for this one.

For the supporting tour and summer festivals, a goatee-bearded Bowie largely made good his promise of no more early hits, playing most of the new album, introducing "Under Pressure" into his set for the first time and barely touching his pre-*Low* material. It was a policy continued in support of the 1997 *Earthling* album which again favored new material—mostly drum'n'bass in style—with occasional album tracks like "The Superman" and "Quicksand".

Left: On July 19, 1997, Bowie and band performed a drum'n'bass set in the Radio One tent at the Phoenix Festival under the name Tao Jones Index. A standard *Earthling* set on the main stage followed the next night.
Above: Bowie wearing the "Earthling" coat designed by Alexander McQueen.

Left: How to celebrate in style: a day after his fiftieth birthday, Bowie hosted a Celebration Concert in aid of Save The Children. Placebo opened the night before a full set from Bowie which included duets with The Pixies' Frank Black, The Cure's Robert Smith, The Foo Fighters, Sonic Youth, and Lou Reed, all pictured (apart from Reed) with the birthday boy below. Madison Square Garden, January 9, 1997.

Right top: "Doctor" Bowie gives the 1999 Commencement Address at the Berklee College of Music as he receives an honorary doctor of music degree. May 8, 1999, Boston, Massachusetts.

Right below: Back doing his day job, Bowie is flanked by collaborators and fellow legends Jagger and Townshend (the Who guitarist played on *Scary Monsters*' "Because You're Young") at Soho's Pop club, following Bowie's performance at the Astoria that evening, December 2, 1999. It was one of only eight concerts in support of new album *"hours…"*.

Everyone Says "Hi"

Celebrations for Bowie's fiftieth birthday at Madison Square Garden were less about reflecting on past glories than advertising his future interests. Judge me on what's new, not what's old, he seemed to be saying. Unfortunately, those judgements were not flattering.

Released in 1999, *"hours…"* was Bowie's least successful UK album in twenty years. Despite a four-star *Billboard* review, its melancholic feel and reliance on string synth melodies failed to interest any but hardcore fans. Even so, tickets to his eight promotional gigs vanished in seconds.

As the new millennium dawned, however, chart positions were the furthest things from Bowie's mind. All he cared about was the birth, on August 15, of his new daughter, Lexi.

Above: Keeping up with the Joneses. With son Duncan a success in the advertising world (*left*), Bowie's personal life became even happier with the birth of daughter Alexandria Zahra Jones (*center*) on August 15, 2000 (pictured here with Iman in New York's SoHo on November 9, 2009).

Above: David Bowie, star and curator of the Meltdown Festival, with Bono and Brian Eno, June 29, 2002.
Opposite: Three decades after arriving at the same port for his Ziggy Stardust tour, David Bowie disembarks the *QE2* in New York City to begin a series of North American Area2 Music Festivals, July 26, 2002.

"The main thing for Brian and me was to make rock and roll absurd. It was to take anything that was serious and mock it."

Never Let Me Down

After the return of Brian Eno on *1.Outside*, it was the turn of Tony Visconti to recreate older magic on 2002's *Heathen*. A strong performer in the US and UK, the album also saw contributions from several other familiar faces: Pete Townshend played on "Slow Burn", Dave Grohl, last seen at Bowie's fiftieth, popped up on "I've Been Waiting For You", while Carlos Alomar and the Borneo Horns from the Serious Moonlight tour were also present. One old name, however, was only there obliquely. The song "I Took A Trip On A Gemini Spaceship" was credited to

Norman Carl Odam, also known as the Legendary Stardust Cowboy—nominally, at least, Ziggy's father.

The Cowboy was also personally invited onto the bill at London's Meltdown Festival by that year's curator —a certain Mr. Bowie. Bowie's own performance at the event saw the *Low* album performed in its entirety followed by all of *Heathen* then "White Light, White Heat", "Fame", "Ziggy Stardust", "Hallo Spaceboy", and "I'm Afraid Of Americans".

It was bold, orchestral—and sold-out in seconds. The following *Heathen* mini-

tour could have played for another year and still have not reached everyone who wanted a ticket.

Meltdown also marked the end to Bowie's "no old hits" policy. The "hours…" mini tour had seen a few favorites sneak back in, but this was the first time in a decade where "Ziggy Stardust" could be heard alongside "Rebel Rebel" and "Space Oddity".

After years of seemingly dodging past glories, Bowie was keen to build on the success of *Heathen*. The *Reality* album and full-scale tour were only months away—and they would be big.

Above: Under the spotlight, the serious spotlight… (*left to right*) At Paris's Le Zenith, September 24, 2002; Wantagh, NY's Jones Beach Theater, August 2; the Move Festival, Old Trafford Cricket Ground, Manchester UK, July 10; at Irvine, CA's Verizon Amphitheater, August 13; and, taking a break from the tour, at the VH1 *Vogue* Fashion Awards at Radio City Music Hall, October 15.

"For me the Eastern leg of a tour is always the carrot. For the rest, however magical the chemistry of the performance, the day—to—day mechanics of getting from city to city are draining and monumentally boring. That's the stick."

Above: Bowie performs live on NBC's *Today Show* as part of the Toyota Concert Series in Rockefeller Plaza, September 18, 2003. Alongside him is Gail Ann Dorsey, not only Bowie's main bass player since 1995's Outside tour, but also backup singer and occasional lead vocalist, notably on "Under Pressure".

Opposite: Performing to an even larger TV audience via satellite link, at London's Riverside Studios, September 8, 2003.

"I've made some gross mistakes, but fortunately I've had nobody to blame but myself. I stopped having managers around 1977."

Above: Back to Reality, back to life. (*left to right*) At Munich's Olympiahalle, October 27, 2003; playing his distinctive white 1956 Supro Dual Tone in Rotterdam, October 15; and headlining the final day of the Isle of Wight Festival, June 13, 2004—weeks before his suspected heart attack.

"I'd rather take a longer time to get somewhere than go by plane. It heightens one's sense of awareness, I think."

Never Get Old

With Bowie energized and recharged in 2003, his new album, *Reality*, was a brasher, more insolent collection of songs. Customary cover versions this time were Jonathan Richman's "Pablo Picasso" and "Try Some, Buy Some" from George Harrison's *Living In The Material World* album, while the title track and "New Killer Star" continued to show that Bowie could still nu-rock with best of his contemporaries. On a more downbeat note, "The Loneliest Guy", "Never Get Old" and "Bring Me The Disco King" took reflection to new and more somber levels.

Kicking off in Denmark on October 7, 2003, the Reality tour once again plundered the back catalog with gusto, notably mixing the hits from *Let's Dance* and *Tonight* with earlier glam classics and newer tracks. Unfortunately, while Bowie's creative stock was strong, his body was not. What was thought to be a pinched nerve in his shoulder during a show at Germany's Hurricane Festival on June 25, 2004, was later diagnosed as an acutely blocked artery. David Bowie, who had seemed to be in the the form of his life during the tour, had suffered a minor heart attack.

Left and right: Five years after curating Meltdown, Bowie was asked to present The H&M High Line Festival 2007, May 9–19. Acts he invited included UK comedian Ricky Gervais (*left*) (whose show, *Extras*, he has appeared in), Laurie Anderson (*right*), The Polyphonic Spree, cabaret queen Meow Meow and, his current favorite act, Arcade Fire.

My Death

Ever since the murder of his good friend John Lennon in December 1980, Bowie has been paranoid about his life being ended before time. Rarely, however, did his nightmares have such a mundane conclusion as mere illness.

2004 was largely given over to recuperation in Bowie's Manhattan home. Work, in the short term, he decided would largely involve other people. After a duet on "Changes" with Butterfly Boucher appeared on the soundtrack to *Shrek 2*, he recorded songs with Brian Transeau, Scarlett Johansson, TV on the Radio, Snoop Dogg, and Danish band Kashmir. His comeback stage appearance took longer to arrive, but on September 8, 2005, Bowie joined Arcade Fire on "Wake Up", "Five Years", and "Life On Mars?" for TV's *Fashion Rocks* event.

Above: A walk on the mild side as Lou
Reed is awarded Syracuse University's
highest alumni award, April 26, 2007.
Opposite: Three days earlier Bowie
joined Bill Clinton at the 2007 Food Bank
of New York Can-Do Awards Dinner
honoring The Edge and Jimmy Fallon.

Above and opposite: In April 2010 Angie Bowie told the *Guardian* newspaper, "I haven't heard from Zowie, or Duncan as he calls himself now, for five years. He e-mailed me but the relationship didn't progress and I think reconciliation is unlikely." Father and son, however, have never been closer.

On January 23, 2009, David joined Duncan (*center*) at the Eccles Theater, Utah, for the Sundance Film Festival premiere of *Moon*, starring Sam Rockwell (*right*)—and directed by Duncan Jones. Among its many accolades, *Moon* earned Duncan a BAFTA for special achievement in his first feature film.

"The most glorious thing that came out of
my last marriage was my wonderful son Joe."

"We took a six-week boat trip up and down the Italian coast. By the end, you are either passionately in love or you can't stand the sight of each other. But for us, it just worked out."

A Better Future

In May 2006 David Bowie turned up on stage with David Gilmour at London's Royal Albert Hall to sing "Comfortably Numb" and "Arnold Layne". A few months earlier he had performed "Changes" with Alicia Keys before singing "Fantastic Voyage" and "Wild Is The Wind" solo at the annual Keep A Child Alive charity dinner in New York. Each performance sent shivers down the audiences' spines and the same question was asked: would Bowie ever tour again? The answer is: we don't know. And the man himself isn't saying. But, as every year goes by since 2003's *Reality* the same rumors arise: he's been working on new material. Is this the month we get to hear it?

Bowie is by no means a recluse but nor does he have the need of, say, Paul McCartney or Rod Stewart, to still be reminding the world of how good he is by continually touring. And Bowie *is* good. Just as good now as he ever was.

The man who invented Aladdin Sane, Major Tom, Ziggy Stardust, Halloween Jack, and the Thin White Duke is still alive and well because, despite his attempts to deceive, David Bowie is all those characters.

Just as they are all part of the man the world once knew as David Jones.

Acknowledgments

My thanks to everyone at Endeavour London: in particular to Charles for giving me a glimpse of the Getty Images archive's rich history, to Jen for her picture mastery and general forbearance, to Ros for making it look so incredible, to Mark for ensuring I sound as knowledgeable as possible, to Kate for thinking of me in the first place and to Denis O'Regan for his photography and insider knowledge. Thanks also to Angela and Raf for their unique support and, of course, to Mr Jones himself, without whom the world—and my iPod—would be considerably emptier.

Jeff Hudson, London May 2010

Picture Credits